everyday
words

Illustrated by Gaunor Berry

My body

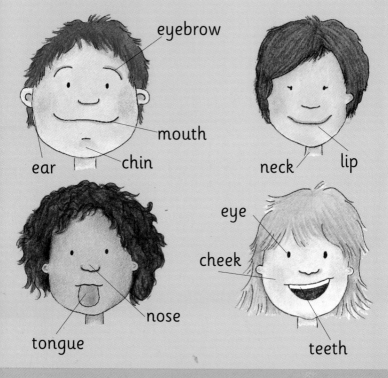

eyebrow

mouth

ear   chin

neck   lip

eye

cheek

nose

tongue

teeth

wash   skip

eat

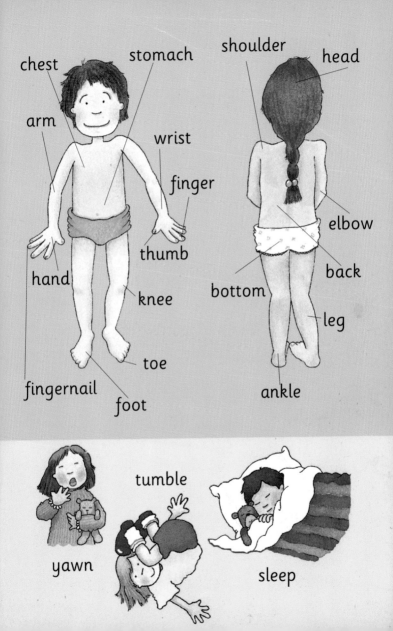

chest
stomach
shoulder
head
arm
wrist
finger
thumb
hand
knee
toe
fingernail
foot
elbow
back
bottom
leg
ankle

yawn
tumble
sleep

Clothes

shorts

mittens

pyjamas

blouse

scarf

shirt

trousers

dress

tie

sweater/
jumper

sandals

boots

slippers

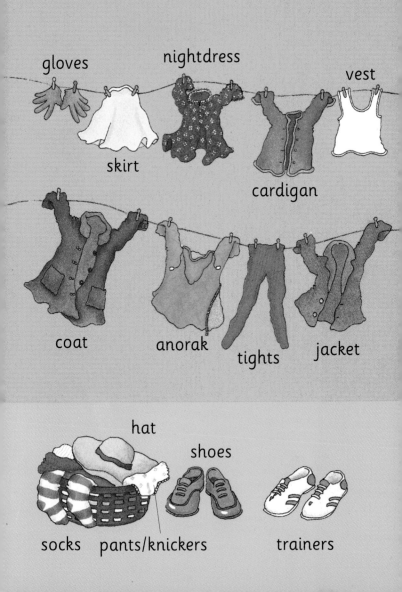

gloves

nightdress

vest

skirt

cardigan

coat

anorak

tights

jacket

hat

shoes

socks

pants/knickers

trainers

Families

granny/grandma   grandad/grandpa

husband   wife

sister brother   baby

uncle

cousin

aunt

twins

mother/mummy

father/daddy

son

daughter

Food

biscuits

milk

chicken

beefburger

ham

eggs

juice

bread

salad

sausages

sauce

cheese

pizza

sugar

spaghetti

meat

sandwiches

jam

fruit

coffee

vegetables

orange

peas

yoghurt

water

cake

apple

tea

nuts

orangeade

Everyday things

envelope

fire

fruit

butterfly

flowers

clock

hammer

bottle

camera

comb

apron

glass

iron   bath   bag

jug   apple   bricks

door   house   doll

box   chair   jar

More everyday things

kettle

leaf

moon

lamp

scissors

picture

paints

table

watch

tin

stars

mirror

television

keys

oven

sun

soap

tools

refrigerator

telephone

ribbon

pencils

book

wheelbarrow

The countryside

fence

forest

insects

cave

ladybird

bridge

river

hill

bees

fields

grass

leaf

worm

sky

windmill

waterfall

tree

mole

snail

hot air balloons

wasps

spider's web

orchard

lane

butterfly

gate

nest

caterpillar

flowers

bird

Doing words

dress

sit

read

write

wash

dry

sing

eat

walk

ride

drink

run

paint

yawn

dance

splash

creep

blow

whisper

wave

jump

cook

smile

shop

Animals

mouse

fish

crocodile

goat

gorilla

cat

lion

turtle

yak

koalas

rabbit

snake

whale

dog

octopus

frog

ducks

wolf

zebra

swan

sheep

panda

tiger

monkey

penguin

elephant

rhino

polar bear

People

explorer

pilot

nurse

actor

optician

dentist

workman

mechanic

detective

florist

baker

doctor

gymnast canoeist acrobat

driver  deep-sea diver  juggler

decorator  artist astronaut

astronomer  butcher

Transport

boat

ambulance

motorcycle

tractor

jeep

aeroplane

helicopter

canoe

racing car

digger

bicycle

submarine

car

train

Shapes and colours

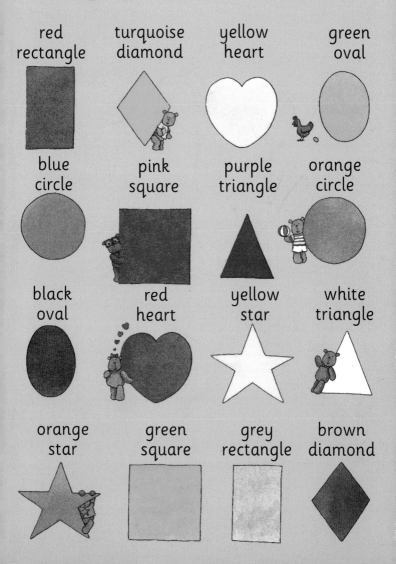

red
rectangle

turquoise
diamond

yellow
heart

green
oval

blue
circle

pink
square

purple
triangle

orange
circle

black
oval

red
heart

yellow
star

white
triangle

orange
star

green
square

grey
rectangle

brown
diamond

Numbers

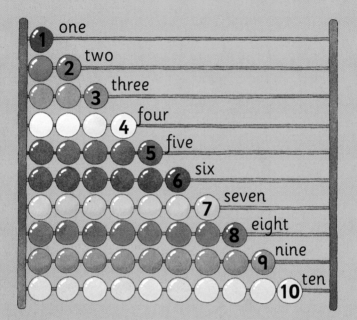

eleven	11	twenty-one	21
twelve	12	thirty	30
thirteen	13	forty	40
fourteen	14	fifty	50
fifteen	15	sixty	60
sixteen	16	seventy	70
seventeen	17	eighty	80
eighteen	18	ninety	90
nineteen	19	one hundred	100
twenty	20		

Weather words

snow

rainbow

sun

rain

thunder and lightning

Days of the week

Sunday
Monday
Tuesday
Wednesday
Thursday
Friday
Saturday

Months of the year

January
February
March
April
May
June
July
August
September
October
November
December

Opposite words

up

down

hot

cold

dirty

clean

old

new

thin

fat

tall

short

Words we write a lot

about	**d**id	her
after	do	here
all	doing	him
am	down	his
an		
and	**f**or	**i**f
are	from	in
as		into
at	**g**et	is
away	getting	it
	go	
back	goes	**l**ike
be	going	look
because	good	looking
but	got	
		made
came	**h**ad	make
can	has	me
come	have	more
comes	having	my
coming	he	myself